INVESTING FOR BEGINNERS

9 Little-Known Investing Strategies to Help You Grow Your Money Effortlessly for Financial Freedom

Michael Henson

Table of Contents

Table of Contents

INTRODUCTION

Being worried about money all the time is stressful. It can prevent you from relaxing in the evening or sleeping well. It can prevent you from getting the health care you need or enjoying fun activities due to the cost.

A lack of money can also have you very worried about your future. Will you have enough money to retire? Will you have to work beyond your physical and mental limits in order to have the money you need? When we think of our golden years, we want to think about being able to live comfortably.

Investing correctly is the key to being able to do so. Very few of us are born into families with unlimited wealth. Most of us also agree we don't have to have an abundance of money. Just enough to meet our needs, to have some fun as we get older, and perhaps to leave to our loved ones.

Investing isn't the same as gambling, and it is very important to know the difference. Investing involves much more than just luck. It involves careful planning, discipline, and applying knowledge. Investing means you follow the market and you continue to try new things.

You have to diversify your portfolio in order to make money. If all of your investments are in one group, you can make money, but what will you do if you lose it?

Investing is about having a safety net in place to help reduce the overall risk. There is no way to completely eliminate the risks, but you can reduce them.

It is a common misconception that you must be an expert in investment planning to do well with it. The truth is you just need to learn the nine secrets that are covered in this book. They are practical, they are possible, and they can help you get results. Investing in a manner that increases your overall wealth can reduce stress and give you peace of mind about your future.

When you explore the history of very successful financial individuals in U.S. history, you will find there are many to whom you can refer. It isn't what they accumulated in wealth that you should focus on, though, as much as it is how they went about making it happen.

Many of these individuals who created vast fortunes started out with very little. They may not have had a formal education or a wealthy family. However, they found a way to create wealth and to leave a legacy behind them.

John Hancock will always be well known as the guy who wrote his name very largely on the Declaration of Independence! However, he grew up the poor son of a minister. He was involved in trading with his uncle, and when he died in 1973, he was worth the equivalent of $79 billion in today's money.

At the young age of 11, Cornelius Vanderbilt quit school and started a ferry service along with his father. This service extended from Manhattan to Staten Island. His father made him a full partner at the age of 16. When he died in 1877, he was worth the equivalent of $157 billion. He invested heavily in railroads and steam ships.

To give you some more recent examples, take a look at the investments, earnings, and overall wealth of Bill Gates and Warren Buffet. Sam Walton is another name worth mentioning. Each of these men had a vision about how to go about making money and giving back to society.

Successful investing is a key part of financial freedom. If you owe money in every direction, it is a heavy burden to carry. It is a dark cloud that lingers in all you do. When you see that debt go away, you can lighten your load. It is important that your investments are ethical and that you never compromise your integrity or character to make some cash.

As you read through this book, you can stop feeling intimidated about investing. You can gain some confidence and formulate ideas about how you will proceed. A solid plan of action is very important for investing so you don't lose your money.

It is true that the earlier in life you start investing the better. However, you need to put that all behind you. Focus on today and where you are right now. It doesn't do you any good to have regrets or self-disappointment if you haven't been successfully investing.

Set your mindset to a positive one and be disciplined. Hold yourself accountable for your investment actions. Taking action is very important too. If you are too worried about failing, you may never get that money into any location.

Putting cash into the bank in savings account is responsible, and that does mean you have money put away for emergency situations. However, that isn't going to be a form of investing. It isn't going to generate a return of your money that helps you grow wealth.

If you are ready to turn things around and to see how you can make your money grow, investing is right for you. Now is the time to turn the page, get a plan in motion, and see the positive results of doing so!

CHAPTER 1
ESTABLISH GOALS AND A PLAN TO REACH THEM

How are you going to measure the success of your investing if you don't have a plan in motion? You must establish goals and then execute them. As you read through this book, take notes and jot down ideas.

When you get done reading the material, use what you have learned to create goals. You need a large overall goal that is very detailed. Next, you need to identify steps that you will take to reach that goal. For the larger steps, break it down into milestones.

Write down your plan of action in as much detail as you can. Your plan may change with time, and that is okay. We will talk about evaluating your plan of action in one of the later chapters of this book.

When it comes to your goals and your plan of action for investing, it isn't set in stone. In fact, it should continue to be a work in progress. As you learn, as the market changes, and as your money grows, you will need to make changes to your plan of action.

KEEP IT REALISTIC

You can't successfully invest and make money if you are chasing rainbows! Keep it realistic so that you can make progress and see success. For example, you can't just say, "I want to become a billionaire," and then do nothing else.

If your goal is truly to be a billionaire, then you need a realistic plan of action for how you will make that happen. It is going to take a considerable amount of time and plenty of aggressive investing.

HOLD YOURSELF ACCOUNTABLE

At the end of the day, you are the only one that can make decisions for investing. Hold yourself accountable, and don't make excuses. If you can admit what you did wrong, where you failed to take action, and what you did right, then you are leaps and bounds ahead of the average person out there.

Be honest with yourself when it comes to investing. If you are afraid, reduce those barriers and face them head-on. If you have failed at investing before, do it better this time around. If you don't have much money with which to work, don't make that an excuse for not investing.

LEARN FROM YOUR MISTAKES

Too many people are afraid to make a mistake with investing. That is why they leave their money in a savings account. They don't want to risk losing any of it. However, they also don't benefit from the possible gains.

In a future chapter, we are going to cover why you should diversify your investments. This is the method that helps you reduce any overall losses and generate significant gains with your investments.

There is no way to predict the market with absolute certainty, so you will have losses. You will make investments that don't pan out, but you will also make those that pay off nicely. Learn from your mistakes and move on; don't beat yourself up over them.

FAILURE TO TAKE ACTION MEANS FAILURE OVERALL

Keep in mind that if you don't invest at all, you have already failed in regards to financial freedom for your future. That is a disappointing thought to consider! You have every opportunity to do well with investing, but you must take one step forward. Take baby steps at first if you must, but keep moving!

A lack of action means you will continue with your current status quo. It is amazing how many people wish their financial circumstances were different yet fail to take action to make those changes become a reality.

Be willing to expand your knowledge about investing. Be willing to spend some time and effort learning and gaining new insight. Be up to the challenges and pursue ways to increase your financial worth!

LOOK AT THE BIG PICTURE

Investing isn't a race to the finish line. It is often slow and steady over the long term. When you are creating your goals and your plan of action, keep the big picture in mind. Where do you want to be a year from now? Five years? Ten years? That time is going to go by faster than you think!

Don't focus your attention only on income return that includes interest and dividends. You also need to think about capital return. This is the money you originally invested, and that is your total overall return.

STICK TO YOUR GOALS

Even if the market gets shaky, don't let that rattle your cage. Have faith in your goals and your marketing methods. Don't let the changes others are making be the reason you change your investing strategies.

Following the pack is easy; standing apart is more difficult. Yet think about the wealthy investors mentioned in the introduction. They didn't follow the crowd. Instead, they learned and they practiced sound principles for investing. They didn't waiver when the market got a bit uncomfortable.

CHAPTER 2
INVEST LOGICALLY, NOT EMOTIONALLY

Why do so many people fail when it comes to investing? They start gambling instead of investing! That desire to have the big windfall of money coming to them can cause all logic to go right out the window. This is the most common mistake that you MUST avoid!

DON'T FOLLOW THE CROWD

Panic and self-doubt can creep in when others are buying or selling. You may not feel that you should, but what if you are wrong? What if all of them are right?

It can get the best of you! With a logical plan of action to follow, you can stay confident in your decision. It may be right and it may be wrong, but you didn't let your emotions get the best of you.

DO YOUR HOMEWORK

If you have done your homework, you can be confident in your investing decisions. You won't be second-guessing yourself and trying to come up with solutions at the last minute. You will remember why you are investing in a certain way. Learning is an ongoing process, though, so don't get too comfortable with what you know.

There is also plenty of information out there that is opinion rather than fact. Yet the way it is promoted and as often as you see it, you may assume it is a fact. Make sure you get your information from credible sources. Otherwise, you will be going in circles.

ACCOUNT FOR UNFORESEEN VARIABLES

If the market were perfect, everyone who invested would be rich. There are unforeseen variables that you can't do anything about. Markets crash, the economy takes a hit, etc.

Keep all of that in mind, but don't get too caught up in it. The "what if" scenario can be what allows emotions to rule rather than sticking to logical investing. What if the investment you didn't make turns out to make money for others? It may happen, and you just have to keep your head up.

What if the fact you didn't sell when everyone else did costs you money in the end? Well, you can't win them all and you just keep your head up! This may sound hard at first, but the more you invest and the more you believe in your investing plan of action, the easier it becomes.

STAY DISCIPLINED

Fighting with others can be stressful, but an internal conflict can be overwhelming. You can't get away from yourself, and it can cause you a great deal of emotional turmoil. Stay disciplined and look over your plan of action for investing.

Think about why you are investing, why you own certain entities, and why you should sell others. If you do this, you will remain in control. Don't make rash or rushed decisions based on others or on changes in the market. Stick to the plan—and if that plan fails to work over time, modify it.

If you didn't develop the best spending and saving habits early in life, then it can be harder for you to be disciplined. You need to have measures in place to ensure you are. Remember, you have to be accountable to yourself. You also need your plan in writing so you can refer to it when you start to feel conflicted.

Don't overlook the fact that our daily choices also influence the amount of capital we have for saving and investing. If you have the mindset of consuming rather than saving, it can be tough. If you haven't differentiated between wants and needs, now is the time to do so.

By postponing consumption so that you can invest, you will have a very strong foundation for the future. If you spend every bit of money you have coming in, that complicates investing.

You may find you have to lay this foundation and integrate it into your thinking before you can go forward with any type of investing. You may have to re-evaluate your current budget and make changes where you can.

SMART GOAL PLANNING

Make sure you cover all of the key points when it comes to goal planning. SMART allows you to have a checklist to which you can refer to in order to make sure you have everything detailed to follow successfully.

- **S**pecific — Be very detailed with what your goals include and how you will achieve them. Write them down!
- **M**easurable — How will you measure your success?
- **A**sk — Get expert advice when you have investment questions.
- **R**esponsibility — Accept your choices and adjust your investing strategy as you need to if evaluations show something is lacking.
- **T**ransparent — Let your friends and family know your goals for investing.

DON'T CHASE THE NEXT BIG THING

"Get rich quick and have all the money you need" is what many people want! However, you can get into a mess if you are chasing the next big thing all the time. Part of the problem is we hear about how much money someone made when they invested in Viagra, Apple, or even Facebook.

It gives us the impression that we should focus on those high-dollar investments. Yet those are the same as finding a needle in a haystack. Sure, you may get lucky, but what if you don't? The best course of action is a solid plan for aggressive investing that will yield generous returns over time.

CHAPTER 3
DIVERSIFY YOUR INVESTMENTS

Diversifying your investments is very important so you don't end up with huge losses. While you want to think positive when you invest and you want to limit your risk, you can't control the market. There are too many variables and too many unknowns.

What you can do, though, is limit the risk and the amount of potential loss incurred. You can do this by diversifying your investments. By spreading them out, you can create a very good portfolio. At the same time, it means you have the best chance of coming out ahead overall with your investments.

RATIO BALANCE

There is a simple ratio balance to keep in mind when it comes to your investment portfolio. It doesn't have to be exact, but you should have it very close to this particular balance.

- 40% in bonds
- 60% in equity

Don't make the mistake of thinking diversifying your investments means you invest in several entities. That is only one part of it. The key piece of diversifying is making sure your portfolio has many investment types that are different from each other.

SEARCH FOR VALUE AND BARGAINS

Allocate some time every week to searching for value and bargains that you can invest in. Don't expect these entities to just fall into your lap. You may hear about them from other investors or on the Internet, but the majority of them you won't.

It isn't until you start spending time researching up-and-coming businesses that this door opens up to you. Don't overlook current businesses that are growing in new directions either.

INVEST WORLDWIDE

It is a very good idea to invest in entities worldwide. If the U.S. economy takes a hard hit, all of your investments can too if that is all you have. However, if you have worldwide investments, it isn't going to be as hard of a hit for you.

The economy around the world has ups and downs at different points. With some diverse investments in different countries, you will be able to benefit from the gains and you won't be hit as hard by the falls either.

LIMIT PROVIDERS

When you determine your profits from investing, you have to subtract any fees you pay. While you need to avoid putting all of your eggs in one basket, so to speak, you should limit providers. The more providers you use, the more you will typically pay in fees.

ASSET CLASSES

Diversify some of your investments in terms of asset classes too. This can help you benefit from any upswings in a given market. However, there could be dips experienced in other markets at the same time. The balance is in place to allow you to keep making money and to not worry about those losses.

CASH IN THE BANK ISN'T INVESTING

If your mindset is "cash in the bank = safety," you are wrong. That equation doesn't make sense when you are trying to achieve financial freedom. Cash in the bank is great for a cushion and to have money for emergency expenses. Cash is also important to have for various needs.

In fact, most experts believe you should have enough cash in the bank to cover your basic living expenses for three months. You never know when you may lose your job or become ill. This money put aside can give you some time to get your health back in order or to find another job.

However, cash in the bank is NOT an investment strategy. It significantly limits your future spending power, and you don't want to hold yourself back like that. There is very little return at all on this type of process due to inflation and taxes.

CHAPTER 4
PREPARE FOR UNPREDICTABLE MARKETS

There is no doubt that it is exciting when you hear that the stock market has gone up by 30% and the economy is doing well. However, even though those are Wall Street figures, you didn't really see a 30% jump in the investments you have out there.

This can be puzzling, but it has to do with the gap between investment returns and investor returns. To help you reduce that gap, you can put a few things into motion. They will also help you prepare for an unpredictable market.

GROW YOUR RETIREMENT FUND

If you have a 401k or IRA for retirement, put as much money into it as you can. These investments are usually on the less aggressive side, but they will still grow your money over time. If your employer matches what you invest, you definitely need to maximize your deposits. His or her portion is free money to you!

INVEST FOR REAL RETURNS

We already talked about why placing all of your cash into your savings account isn't the best option for growing your returns. You can't be entirely conservative with your investments either. You may think doing so reduces your risk in an unpredictable economic time, but it also hinders your chance to make any real profits on your investments.

BEAR AND BULL MARKETS

The market can be calm with very few changes at times. The ups and downs are moderate, but that isn't the normal data for the market. As you learn about investing, you will also learn it isn't time to jump ship just because the market dips.

One of the surest ways to miss out on investment gains is to sell when the market seems to be getting difficult. Familiarize yourself with the normal ups and downs of the market and you will feel more comfortable sticking to your overall investment strategy and plan of action.

A bull market is when there is a rise in the profits from investments. The value of investments may be anticipated to rise, and that means more people are rushing to buy them.

With a bear market, there is a drop in profits from investments. The value of investments may be anticipated to drop, and that means more people are rushing to sell them.

Avoid getting yourself really mixed up in those terms or those actions. If your portfolio is well-diversified, you will be able to take a few hits when there is a bearish market and it won't drop your investment value overall.

BE PERSISTENT

Very few people find that investing is always a smooth course. There can be some rough waters that emerge. You need to have your life jacket on and your life boat ready. There are peaks and valleys and highs and lows for which to prepare.

Yet investing successfully is a long-term journey, and the cycle is going to have plenty of good times along with some rough patches. Your patience and determination are going to be tested again and again.

Your ability to use logic instead of emotion for investment decisions will play a vital role in how you come out in the end. If you are determined and you have a positive attitude, though, you will be able to weather those storms until the sun shines again.

Don't let the setbacks get the best of you; they don't mean you have failed. Too many people start to second-guess themselves because of unpredictable elements of the market. Don't get discouraged and give up.

DON'T PANIC

The fear of losing money you have invested, or funds your money has earned through investing, can cause panic. With a long-term approach to your investment strategy, you can ignore those day-to-day issues that Wall Street reports.

You can avoid those trigger-happy investment decisions that will get the best of you in the overall scheme of things. Sometimes you have to stay with a given stock for five years or longer to see it generate a nice profit for you.

CHAPTER 5
LAW OF ATTRACTION FOR WEALTH ACCUMULATION

The Law of Attraction for wealth accumulation is important. Do you know people who always seem to invest in the right things? Who always come out on top of the game? They aren't lucky; they use the Law of Attraction to their benefit!

You can too, and it is going to bring you to your ultimate goal of financial freedom. To do so, you must embrace the opportunities to change your life and your finances for the better. You can increase your wealth, or you can remain a slave to your debts. The power is in your hands, but most people don't think it is.

CAUSE AND EFFECT

While none of us can control everything in our lives, we can usually control cause and effect through our actions. For every action, there is a reaction. If you fail to take action, there is no reaction, and that doesn't help you reach your goals either.

Focus your efforts on accumulating wealth and not accumulating liabilities. Spend time learning more about money management and investing. Think about cause and effect as you are taking part in something. If you want a particular effect, what can you do to make that possible?

BELIEVE YOU CAN DO IT

If you don't believe you can achieve financial freedom, it will always elude you. Encourage yourself and really focus on what you have done well. Your plan of action needs to be a challenge but not unachievable. Open your eyes and your mind to new financial growth possibilities. Doing the same old thing but expecting better results isn't realistic.

If you notice negative thoughts getting into your mind, replace them with positive ones. You may have to focus on this a great deal, and it takes discipline. However, in time, you can retrain your thought process, and then you will have to redirect your thoughts less and less.

What you expect to happen is often what will happen. When you get up in the morning, focus on the outcome you want. When you go to bed at night, let the scenario play out in your mind. During the day, take actions that will get you those results.

The higher the expectations you have for yourself and your life, the more likely it is that you will accumulate great wealth over time through your investment habits.

Remember, you must take action to turn those dreams into reality.

THE LAW OF ATTRACTION

Many people have heard of the Law of Attraction and how it relates to getting the mate you want and deserve. However, the law of attraction also applies to financial freedom. You need to attract people in your life that have similar goals and plans of action.

If you want to change your life, you need to change what goes on around you. If you are surrounded by people who don't like their financial situation and complain but do nothing, that is the lifestyle you are going to have too.

The amount of quality information you will receive through others is hard to measure. You can share those details with others, and they can share with you. When you are around people that have the same mindset as you do, it helps encourage you to work towards your goals even more.

THE LAW OF CORRESPONDENCE

The Law of Correspondence goes along with this too. You can't ignore the outside world and just focus on you and your needs. That is going to be a lonely existence without any real value to you. A quality life is one you enjoy but that you also share with others.

You also have to correspond with your own inner thoughts. You can't get what you want if you don't internally feel that you deserve it. Don't feel guilty about your desire to have more financial wealth or about your decision to go after it.

THE LAW OF ABUNDANCE

We live in a world where the more people have, the more they think they are happy. The truth is they aren't, because they are worried about the mortgage on that home or the car payment due on that fancy vehicle. Yet they look good, right?

Living within your means is a very important part of financial freedom. By cutting out many of the unnecessary things in your life, you can still be happy and have a great lifestyle. It reduces financial stress and it also gives you more money for investing.

As your investments grow, it is fine to treat yourself to things you want, as long as you can afford them. In fact, that can be a strong motivator for you to continue with your investing strategy and diversify your portfolio. The truth is there is more than enough money out there for anyone who wants it enough.

THE LAW OF EXCHANGE

Even before we actually had currency in the world, people would engage in the Law of Exchange. This concept involves doing something of value in exchange for something else of value. Make sure the value you get through your investments and work offers you a proportional reward.

To make money, you must increase the value of what you offer from the point of view of others. Continue to improve what you offer and you will find you get more financial gain from it. This is why diversifying your portfolio is such an important part of being successful.

All of us have the same amount of time in any given day to work with. No matter where you live, what you do, or your financial worth, you don't get more than twenty-four hours to work with. However, you can benefit by balancing your time and making sure the efforts you do put forth are productive.

THE LAW OF CONSERVATION

If you want to attract money and grow it for financial freedom, you have to keep what you make. If you spend the investment funds as quickly as you make them, there is no real wealth accumulating. Poor money management can sabotage your efforts so make a disciplined plan and stick to it.

Accumulate assets so you have equity and money you can count on. However, make sure your expenses don't grow at the same rate as your investment returns or you really won't be financially better off in the end.

THE LAW OF INVESTING

According to the Law of Investing, you should put as much time into learning about investments as you would earning the money you invest. This helps ensure you lower your risk of losing large sums of money.

Only work with investment experts who have a proven track record. Don't be shy about asking them for information that verifies they can do the job extremely well. Your investments are too important to entrust to just anyone.

Research them and find a great match. They should also be someone with whom you can communicate well. Over time, your investments will accumulate returns for you. They may be small at first, but they will be there, so don't get discouraged. Don't be in a rush to sell entities either when the market hits a tough patch.

CHAPTER 6
BE WILLING TO TAKE RISKS

You can't make money without investing it, and that requires some risk. There is a significant difference between taking risks and being reckless with your investing. A risk that is acceptable is one that stems from unknown market changes that you can't predict or control.

Reckless and careless risks stem from following get-rich-quick schemes or by not doing your homework. If an investment seems too good to be true, it is. Trust your gut instinct too and don't invest in something that doesn't seem legitimate. Even if you can't put your finger on the problem, it's better to walk away.

CALCULATED RISKS

The concept behind calculated risks is you continue to learn. Then you take that information and apply it to your plan of action. You have lowered the risks because you aren't making common mistakes that cost you money.

A calculated risk is one you take based on applying the best information you have at any given point in time.

In hindsight, it may not turn out to be the best option, but you can still feel good about your decisions.

KNOWLEDGE IS POWER

When it comes to successful investing, knowledge is power. The more you know, the easier it is to see what you are doing well and what you need to improve. The quality of your information matters, so be very selective about where it comes from.

You don't have to be an expert to do very well with investing. However, you do need to pay attention to changes and learn the basics. You can build a great foundation from that basic information. Over time, you can start to branch out with your investments using what you have learned.

POSITIVE ATTITUDE

You can't do well with investing if you are negative. Don't get too hard on yourself when things don't turn out the way you had hoped. Don't give up and take all of your money out of investments either. You need to stay focused and disciplined.

A positive attitude makes you a winner in life. We can't control a lot of what happens every day. However, we can make a decision to handle it with grace. Think about the good things your investments are doing for you rather than being focused on the negative.

If you are diversifying your portfolio like you should, there will always be plenty of positive angles to think about. You will be making money overall, and that is what is important. It is the right way to see financial freedom in your future!

LEARN FROM MISTAKES

Ask any successful investor out there, and they will tell you story after story about investing mistakes they made. So how did they come out on top? According to George Soros, it is all about recognizing those mistakes and turning them around.

If you make a mistake, learn from it, benefit from it, and change it. If you continue to make the same mistake over and over, though, it is no longer just a mistake. It is a choice—a very poor choice, but a choice just the same.

Soros is a Hungarian emigrant who grew up very poor. He created an international hedge fund that is now worth more than $22 billion. He says he is proud of that success but still makes investment mistakes regularly.

TAKE ACTION

Successful investing requires a series of choices. You must take action if you are going to succeed. Don't let the ever-changing world of investing hold you back. If you fear the consequences, the only option you have is failure.

Take action, take a chance, and see how it turns out. Sometimes the risk you take means a portion of what you invested is gone. However, there is also the opportunity for the investment to do far better than you ever imagined.

Learning when to hold on to investments and when to let them go isn't easy. It all goes back to having a very solid investing strategy and focusing on your logical, rather than emotional, connection to those investments.

PAST RETURNS DON'T PREDICT THE FUTURE

A common mistake with investing is assuming past returns will always predict the future outcomes. If that were true, everyone would be making a ton of money from their investments. They would simply sit down with some old years of data and invest money without a second thought.

This type of approach is often referred to as the "buy high, sell low" concept. Anytime equity seems to be doing well, people want to dump more money into them. When it starts to crash, though, they are scrambling to pull their money back out.

Don't get caught up in the performance aspect of investing as that won't help you with taking risk that pays off. You can't time the market, so give up trying. Don't jump in, bail out, and then wait for the right time to jump back in.

Allow a quality investment to do well over the long run and it will make you money. The tip here is to make sure you do your homework. Invest wisely in good entities and you won't have to worry when they take a dip now and then.

RISK TOLERANCE

Before you dive into investing, you need to think about your own risk tolerance. Any good investor realizes how much they can afford to lose. Part of your overall goal and strategy should be how much you need to have at the end of the year.

That dollar amount can help you to set your investing goals appropriately. If you need a small amount of return, you can put 80% of your money in safe entities and only 20% into riskier investments. However, if you must get a higher return, you need to invest more in riskier investments that you have carefully researched.

While it is true you earn more of a return on risky investments, you can also lose more that way. Identify the threshold where you can afford to lose. This definitely needs to be a part of your overall investing strategy for it to work in your favor.

PROFILING INVESTMENTS

It can be tempting to invest in the companies you hear about the most. Yet just because they are talked about in the news, on social media sites, and through other means doesn't make them a wise investment of your money.

It is recommended that you look for companies with at least $50 million market cap. This means the dividend is going to be about twice as much as the S&P 500s dividend yield. Take a look at working capital calculations too in order to really identify the overall financial health of a given company.

CHAPTER 7
COMPOUNDING WEALTH

As you start to see returns on your long-term investments, your overall wealth is going to continue to grow. This doesn't mean you rush out and buy a $100,000 car or take lavish vacations. You can use some of your equity money to pay for things you need or something you really want.

For example, you may still have a mortgage on your home. The amount of interest that you will pay before it is paid off can be very high. It may be a good time to take some of your investment earnings and pay off your mortgage.

Then you can use those savings each month to invest even more. You will have equity in your home, so it is going to be an asset to you as well.

INVEST IN GOLD

Even though the U.S. dollar continues to go through cycles regarding what it is truly worth, gold value is very high. It is a good idea to invest in gold because it doesn't depreciate due to inflation or other factors.

CONTINUE TO LEARN

Don't get too comfortable where you are when it comes to compounding your wealth. Continue to learn, continue to grow, and continue to diversify your portfolio. As you make more money, you will have more to invest.

You can learn about additional forms of investing, including those that are on a global scale. You can also consider putting some of your money into riskier investments as your risk threshold may be increased with more money in your corner. The world of investing always changes and has something new to offer. Stay on top of it and apply what you learn.

AUTOMATE THE PROCESS

As you tweak your investing strategy, you will notice it works better and better. You will be fine-tuning it less frequently. When you get to this point, automate the process as much as you can. There are some forms of investment tasks that can be time-consuming for you to do manually.

They include dividend reinvesting and rebalancing your entities. You need to keep your portfolio tidy and well-diversified. Otherwise, you have careless risks that can reduce your progress towards overall financial freedom.

Such details should never be left to chance, though. It may be a good idea to hire an investment manager to help you out. They should be doing this for you without any extra fees.

KNOW THE FEES INVOLVED

The idea is to make as much money as you can through your investments. Your overall return is your investment less fees. The higher your fees are, the less money you earn toward financial freedom.

Therefore, you should focus on the best diversification plan for your investments with the lowest costs involved. Managed funds do have higher fees with them, but they aren't always going to perform the best.

Always become familiar with any taxes or fees associated with any investment option before you commit to it. The overall cost should be calculated into your decision-making process. If they're not, those fees and taxes can take a huge chunk of the money, and that is frustrating.

When you calculate investment fees, you need to look at trading costs, management fees, and the tax repercussions. Make sure you read the fine print too so you aren't blindsided by hidden fees or costs.

REDUCE YOUR TAX LIABILITY

Death and taxes are inevitable, but that doesn't mean they have to make you miserable. Take care of your health and it will benefit your mind and body; take care to reduce your tax liability and it will support your financial health.

Learn about different investment account types, as some of them offer substantial tax benefits. For example, you can set up an IRA and pay taxes on what you contribute. Yet you won't have to pay any taxes on the growth of such investments.

With a 401k, you can avoid paying taxes when you invest, but you will have to pay those taxes when you withdraw the funds after you retire. To make it all work to your advantage, try to put money into bonds and other entities that offer you tax deferment options.

If you put your money into taxable accounts, you will be giving the IRS anywhere from 20% to 30% more than you have to each year. That is money that could remain in your own pocket, so don't let them have it!

CHAPTER 8
EVALUATE YOUR INVESTMENTS EVERY SIX MONTHS

Don't micromanage your investments or you will drive yourself crazy! It is also going to be hard to stay disciplined and rely on logic rather than emotions.

However, the world of investments changes often. Therefore, you should evaluate your investments every six months. This is your time to make some changes to your investment strategy if you have identified elements that aren't working for you.

WHAT DO YOU OWN?

Your evaluation should include what you own. Think about how it pertains to your overall goals for financial freedom. You need to know everything that is in your portfolio. You also need to examine if it is diversified enough.

WHY DO YOU OWN IT?

What you own isn't nearly as important as why you own it. All successful investors can tell you why they are involved in each and every investment in their portfolio. They don't just have a bunch of random investments.

REVIEW CHANGES IN THE MARKET

What changes have occurred in the market in that six-month period? How have they affected your investment strategy? What is the positive or negative outcome? Were there variables you had control over but overlooked? If so, now is the time to make changes that eliminate those problems.

BE THOROUGH

You need to be both thorough and objective when it comes to your reviews. Don't bypass this six-month review because your investments are making you money. If they are, that is terrific, but identify why they are making money.

There may be some small pitfalls too that you can eliminate. Even if you are making money, are those pitfalls preventing you from making more money? For example, are you paying too much in fees or taxes that could have been money in your own pocket?

EVALUATE SUCCESS

Don't just assume your investments are doing well; you need to evaluate them every six months. This will help you determine your next moves and any changes you may need to implement. Measuring investment performance may seem difficult at first, but it doesn't have to be. It will get easier and easier over time.

YIELD

Take a close look at the yield, a way to measure the income your investments have paid during a given period of time. This is typically a year, so you will just divide it in half for the six-month evaluation. Once you have that amount, divide it by the price of the investment.

RETURN

The return is all of the money you either made or lost on a given investment in that window of time. Take the change in value (positive or negative) from the time of purchase. To determine the return percentage, divide the change plus income by the amount of the original investment.

CAPITAL GAINS AND LOSSES

If you make money by selling a capital asset for more than you paid, that is considered a capital gain. If you sell it for less than you paid, that is called a capital loss. These pieces can be a factor in your portfolio performance, so make sure you don't overlook evaluating them.

UNDERSTANDING YOUR STATEMENTS

You will get statements regularly about your investments, but if you don't understand the information on them, they don't do you any good. They don't present you with data you can use for your performance review.

Statements from different investments can be designed differently, but they all have the same basic information. If you don't understand the information on a given statement, contact the provider and ask them to walk you through it.

In time, it will become easier for you to read that information. It is a learning process, so give it time. Keep your statements so you can reference them too. Comparing a current statement with the last couple can help you see the changes in a given investment.

UPDATE GOALS AND STRATEGY

Based on your findings in that review, you can update your goals and your strategy. Perhaps you have discovered you will make much more than you had anticipated for the year. Then you can set a new goal and continue to challenge yourself.

If you need to make some changes to your investing strategy, now is the time to make it happen. Put those changes into writing so you are familiar with them. Make sure you don't slip into old habits if you get stressed.

CHAPTER 9
BEWARE OF SCAMS

The problem with some investments is they are nothing more than scams. They take advantage of innocent people who are trying to make money the right way. If you are going to invest, you have to be diligent against any such scams out there.

ADVANCED FEES

A common scam is giving you the impression that an investment is legitimate. However, they want you to give them money to give you the opportunity to be involved in that investment opportunity. You should never pay any advanced fees for investing. These scammers take your money, and it is never invested.

OFFSHORE INVESTING

Avoid offshore investing options that tell you it is easy money and that you don't have to pay taxes. You don't know who is behind such scams. They can result in you losing a lot of money. They give you the promise that you will get large gains due to the offshore entities and no tax liability. However, they simply disappear with your money.

PONZI SCHEME

Make sure you don't get your money tied up with a Ponzi Scheme or Pyramid Scheme. Basically, the people running them get your money and funds from many other people. They keep people involved because they pay some small dividends at first to make you think it is moving in the right direction.

However, they are simply taking money from other investors and paying small amounts of it to people who have already invested before them. Some very wealthy investors and even celebrities have fallen victim to such scams.

PUMP AND DUMP

Be careful buying into a rush deal on low-priced stock. They are often promoted as the next thing that will really take off. The people promoting them actually own a large amount of stock in that particular business. The more investors by stock, the higher the value of the shares becomes.

However, there will be a peak when all of a sudden that investor will sell their shares and the value in the market will take a huge fall. The result is you and other investors now have investments in stocks that aren't worth anything at all.

NOT REPORTING INVESTMENTS ON YOUR TAXES

All income has to be reported on your taxes. Some forms of investing have tax breaks or you pay taxes when you access the funds for retirement. It is your responsibility to know how that works for given investments. You may find hiring a tax specialist to file on your behalf is the best route to take.

Don't listen to any brokers or other individuals who may tell you not to report your investments on your taxes. The IRS has more ways to learn about such investments than you can imagine. It will catch up with you and then you will have fines, penalties, and other amounts due to them.

CONCLUSION

Most people don't have extremely high-paying jobs or a wealthy family to give them money. Instead, they have to work hard for what they have. It isn't easy to have money for necessities, for fun, and to put away for the future.

Without good investments, it can be very stressful when it comes to finances. It gets to be very upsetting to always worry about money. Long-term investing can help you have the funds you need for the type of lifestyle you want in the future.

Investing is much more than just randomly putting money into this stock or that bond. It has to do with carefully researching the market and finding good options for your money. Some investments are higher risk than others, yet they offer a better return.

High-risk investments aren't unwise, but you do have to take a calculated risk to make them work. Understanding the fundamentals of investing and being logical with your decision-making process are important.

You can't be in a rush to make a fast buck if you want to have overall financial freedom. Instead, you have to ride out the tough times to enjoy the good times. You can't just rely on past data and believe that is what will occur in the future.

There is always a risk involved with investing; there is no way around that. Yet you can reduce your risk by continuing to learn and evaluate your investing strategy.

Mistakes are going to occur, and some good investments will slip through your fingers now and then. However, if you have diversified your portfolio well, there is absolutely no reason why your returns won't outweigh any losses.

Investing doesn't have to be intimidating, and you don't have to be an expert. You don't have to become a day trader or have all the answers. You do have to invest both time and money to make it work out favorably.

Watch out for potential scams and always research the business before you buy any stocks or bonds that they offer. Think about the future of that business and what it can do. Think about your own marketing strategy and goals too because the amount of money you want to make influences your investing decisions.

The returns on your investments are what really matter. Pay close attention to fees, including taxes you will need to pay on various forms of investing. Make a commitment to long-term success and don't be negative when you have some hard hits now and then.

It is possible for you to achieve financial freedom through your investing strategies and persistence. It doesn't matter how old you are or how much money you currently make. It doesn't matter what your education is. Your mindset, though, does influence the outcome, so always think positive.

Learn from your experiences, both the good and the bad, when it comes to investing. These nine strategies to help you grow your money really do work. However, they all work with each other. They are like pieces of a puzzle. If one or more of them is missing, the big picture doesn't turn out the way it was meant to.

DID YOU LIKE "INVESTING FOR BEGINNERS"?

Before you go, I'd like to say thank you so much for purchasing my book.

I know you could have picked from dozens of books on this subject, but you took a chance with mine and I'm truly grateful for that.

So, once again, a big thanks for downloading this book and reading all the way to the end—I truly appreciate it.

Now I'd like to ask for a small favor if you don't mind . . .

Would you be so kind as to take a minute of your time and leave a review for this book on Amazon?

This feedback will help me continue to write the kind of books that help you get results. And if you loved it, then please feel free to let me know! :)

www.ingramcontent.com/pod-product-compliance
Lightning Source LLC
Chambersburg PA
CBHW071005180526
45168CB00003B/1291